THE BEST OF

2012

MATTHEW PRITCHETT
studied at St Martin's School of Art in
London and first saw himself published
in the *New Statesman* during one of its
rare lapses from high seriousness. He has
been the *Daily Telegraph*'s front-page
pocket cartoonist since 1988. In 1995,
1996, 1999, 2005 and 2009 he was the
winner of the Cartoon Arts Trust Award
and in 1991, 2004 and 2006 he was
'What the Papers Say' Cartoonist of the
Year. In 1996, 1998, 2000, 2008 and
2009 he was the *UK Press Gazette*
Cartoonist of the Year and in 2002 he
received an MBE.

Own your favourite Matt cartoons.
Browse the full range of Matt
cartoons and buy online at
www.telegraph.co.uk/photographs
or call 020 7931 2076.

'It's one of the earliest
examples of builders
flouting local
planning laws'

The Daily Telegraph

THE BEST OF

MATT

2012

An Orion Paperback

First published in Great Britain in 2012 by Orion Books
A division of the Orion Publishing Group Ltd
Orion House
5 Upper Saint Martin's Lane
London, WC2H 9EA

A Hachette UK Company

10 9 8 7 6 5 4 3 2 1

© 2012 Telegraph Media Group Limited

The right of Matthew Pritchett to be identified as the author
of this work has been asserted in accordance with the
Copyright, Designs and Patents Act 1988.

All rights reserved. No part of this publication may be reproduced,
stored in a retrieval system or transmitted in any form or by any means,
without the prior permission in writing of the publisher, nor to be
otherwise circulated in any form of binding or cover other than that in
which it is published without a similar condition, including this
condition, being imposed on the subsequent purchaser.

A CIP catalogue record for this book
is available from the British Library.

ISBN: 978 1 4091 2156 5

Printed in the UK by CPI William Clowes, Beccles NR34 7TL

The Orion Publishing Group's policy is to use papers that
are natural, renewable and recyclable products and
made from wood grown in sustainable forests. The logging
and manufacturing processes are expected to conform to
the environmental regulations of the country of origin.

www.orionbooks.co.uk

'Stay still! I think you've got the God particle in your eye'

THE BEST OF
MATT
2012

'GONE BUST? Is that the tour operator or the country?'

'The taramasalata has really hit the fan now'

Euro Crisis

'I'm counterfeiting euros.
If I'm caught I'll
plead insanity'

'I must say, these bailouts
are very moreish'

'A ratings agency
downgraded my hat'

'It's a triple A battery.
I'm reminding the French
of our credit rating'

US Troops Cause Offence

'There was a huge wasp and my attempts to organise an orderly exit sparked panic'

'It's no longer "if" I have another ouzo, it's "when"'

Greece to leave?

Euro Crisis

'It's so serious that Berlusconi has invited economists to his villa this weekend'

'Double dip is the new dip'

'It's an authentic Italian restaurant. There's no choice – an EU technocrat tells you what you're getting'

EU imposes new leadership

Euro Crisis

'One bulb goes out and the
whole thing is useless.
It's like the euro'

'We are from planet Earth.
We need to borrow a
lot of money'

Double Dip

'These credit rating
people are a nuisance'

'The politicians promised
us that only our children
would suffer'

'If the economy crashes
we could always claim for
whiplash injuries'

Quantitative Easing

'A message from your
accountant, my lord –
a mansion tax is
looking less likely'

'What a big tax bill
you have grandma'

Budget

'I've been talking to my tax adviser – move all my pasties offshore'

'Revenge is a dish best served warm, but not heated up ...'

Pasty tax

'I'm worried this is sending
out an anti-business message'

'Miliband can't call us
a "bad" company now'

'I told my parents you're a Scientologist, but I didn't dare mention you're also a banker'

'Guess which cup your money is under ...'

'And your mother called to say you should be in jail'

'I might need some bail money, Granny, so I'm going to have to sell you'

Libor crisis

Banker Bashing

'I love it when you put on an old suit and find £5 million in the pocket'

'I've half a mind not to give that rogue trader a bonus'

Bonus Culture

Bankers asked to show restraint

Computer glitches

'I don't even want the party I voted for to win'

'It's the Apathy Spring'

Q. Would you like to embarrass and annoy Nick Clegg again?

'I won't have to eat a pasty, will I?'

Lords Reform

'Nick Clegg wants more thistles, nettles and dandelions to get into the Chelsea Flower Show'

'Our daughter wants to go to Oxbridge, so we've got her a Cockney tutor'

Equalities Tsar appointed

Hacking

'In the future everyone will
be hacked for 15 minutes'

'Courtship, mating, laying
eggs –Attenborough's always
there with a camera crew'

'You never remember anything, it's like living with James Murdoch'

'Before we go in, I must warn you, he doesn't know about Father Christmas'

Murdoch pleads ignorance

'Daddy, does the Leveson inquiry go on forever and ever?'

'We're not having lunch with Rebekah Brooks, we're arresting her'

THE LEVESON INQUIRY

'Yes, sugar lumps did change hands ...'

Police lend Rebekah Brooks a horse

Hacking

Cameron's links to News International

Closed Trials

Police

It's OK to swear ...

Pensions

'A few nice days and then it's all over – that's my pension, not the summer'

'We've handled your pension for many years and it has enormous sentimental value'

'Try not to think about my
gold-plated pension while I
take your blood pressure'

Border Control

'Let's relax border controls for health and safety reasons'

Queues

Teachers

'Pay attention!
We're not doing this
for our own benefit'

'I heard you've been
sacked, sir, so I suppose
this is "bonjour"'

'It's not close to a school, but
there are three very good
petrol stations in the area'

'I heard the snow warning
and panic-bought a
team of huskies'

Fuel panic

'I was on my way to panic buy stamps when I ran out of petrol'

'I'm not watering my garden; I'm siphoning petrol'

'It's much cheaper if you travel at a different time – the 1950s for example'

'Move right down inside the wallet'

The Railways

'Can I pay for my
season ticket with this
copper cable?'

Metal thieves

'This looks like a nice spot'

'Farming Today has been replaced by Builders' World'

Planning Laws

'When the planning laws change we're hoping to release them into the wild'

'Tonight on Downton Abbey, 50 new houses are built on the front lawn'

'I'm a traditionalist.
I still believe one of the
people getting married
should be pregnant'

'I went to a gay wedding;
it was like a heterosexual
one, but with a more
expensive present list'

Gay Marriage

'You're a bridesmaid at a heterosexual weddding? That is SO last year'

'It's more serious than I thought – you've got gay bats'

Droughts and Floods

'It's the perfect crime – I'll water your garden and you can water mine ...'

'There's no water'

'Your water butt just sailed away'

Droughts and Floods

'Look, the Shard'

'We're building a
roof over Britain'

'Would you like a leaflet on
conserving water?'

'We collected the rainwater
from the jubilee coverage
to use on our garden'

Diamond Jubilee

JUBILEE PAGEANT SET

SOUVENIR DIAMOND JUBILEE RAIN

'A Lancaster, four Spitfires
and a Hurricane. Shall I
let 'em have it, Sarge?'

'As a tribute to the Queen's
lifetime of service, I'm taking
the rest of the week off'

Olympics

'My imaginary friend works for G4S'

'We forgot to train any sniffer dogs'

Olympics

'The headmistress will be
shooting down any
suspicious aircraft'

'I thought I didn't care
about the Games, but it's
hard not to get swept up in
the wave of cynicism'

'The Olympic remote control
is on the final leg
of its journey'

OLYMPIA 776 BC

WATCH THE
GAMES ON
OUR GIANT
VASES

'Are you sure that was beach volleyball?'

'You should have thought of that before you cycled in an Olympic lane, Mr Wiggins'

'COME ON, whoever you
are, keep doing whatever
you're doing. YESSS! NO
...have we won?'

'I was inspired by the
Olympics. I sold my bike
and bought a bigger TV'

Olympics

'He was watching the showjumping when he fell at the final fence'

'The TV is broken. I've been watching for 20 minutes and we haven't won a gold medal'

'London is full of happy, smiling people; I feel like a stranger in my own city'

Olympics

'I was wrong – it really
did kill him to say the
Olympics were a success'

CLOSING
CEREMONY

'And Her Majesty will be
fired from this cannon . . .'

'Would you mind if some medical students watched me refuse to treat you?'

'The doctor's on strike, so I had his stitches done by the vet'

And finally...

NEW SNOOPING POWERS

'If it's not "morally wrong" could I have a cup of tea with four sugars?'

Paying cash morally wrong

'Typical! I've found the
Higgs boson, but I've
lost my glasses again'

'I don't have a complaint.
I'm just here because
it's so lovely and warm'

And finally...

Camerons leave child in pub

'It's bedtime. Leave your camp or Mummy will Taser you'

Dale Farm

'Don't kiss it better. I want you to refer me to a personal injury lawyer'

And finally...

And finally...

'*Send in Dr Who, please*'

BBC cuts

'LOOK OUT!'

And finally...

'Emperor, I have bad news about your Facebook shares'

PROCESSED
MEAT
PART OF YOUR
SEVEN-A-WEEK

'Could the person monitoring my internet use remind me of my password?'

'We require three 'A's:
A visa
A few C grades
A cheque for £14,000'

And finally...

CROSS CHANNEL FERRIES

PART OF THE WORK EXPERIENCE PROGRAMME

'This is my husband's study, or as I call it, the drunk tank'

TODAY

RANGERS FC
ADMINISTRATORS

V

PORTSMOUTH FC
ADMINISTRATORS

'Gentlemen, Iran's very first
long range nuclear
power station'

And finally...

'New employment laws
mean we can get rid of
Sleepy and Dopey'

'Don't just stand there –
put up prices!'

'There's never a metal thief around when you need one'

'We apologise for the non-arrival of your bonus. This is due to the Prime Minister throwing himself in front of it'

And finally...

'I'm thinking of boiling the kettle. What's your best price?'

BlackBerry BREAKDOWN

'I'M ON THE TRAIN'